The Big Book of Questions & Answers

Sinclair B. Ferguson

CF4•K

To
MARK and FIONA
For
LINDSAY and ANDREW

Copyright © Sinclair B. Ferguson

Published by Christian Focus Publications,
Geanies House, Fearn, Tain, Ross-shire,
IV20 1TW, Scotland, U.K.

e-mail:info@christianfocus.com
www.christianfocus.com

Published in 1997
Reprinted 1998, 1999, 2000, 2003, 2005, 2007, 2009

Illustrations by Diane Matthes
Cover preparation by Douglas McConnach

ISBN 978-1-85792-295-0

Scripture quotations are from *The New International Version*,
© 1973, 1978, 1984 by the International Bible Society.

Printed by Bell and Bain, Glasgow

Mixed Sources
Product group from well-managed
forests and other controlled sources
www.fsc.org Cert no. TT-COC-002769
© 1996 Forest Stewardship Council
FSC

CONTENTS

FOR PARENTS OR LEADERS

In order to help you get the most out of this material we have supplemented the text by giving suggestions for activities. These aim to help the child understand the ideas being presented.

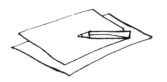 Write down / compile information / keep a diary

 Think about the issues being talked about, possibly leading to action being taken.

 Draw a poster / make something / be creative. A special notebook and a supply of paper for posters will help here.

 Take some action! Possibly providing support through prayer or practical help.

 Find out information from the Bible or other relevant reading material.

 A short prayer is given to bring the activities to a close.

 Short passages from the Bible for further reading are suggested.

  Short questions are given to encourage thought and discussion of the questions and answers.

Do you have lots of questions?

* Sometimes teachers can tell us the answers.
* Sometimes others can help us.
* Sometimes we find out the answer ourselves by reading a book or watching a television programme.

But we have many questions that only God can answer.

Perhaps you never ask these questions out loud. But you ask them inside. You think about them when you are on your own. Sometimes you lie awake in bed thinking about them.
Where can you find the answers?

God answers our questions in his special book, the Bible. *The Big Book Of Questions and Answers* will help you to find out what his answers are.

Enjoy this book and the activities which Ruth Maclean has helped to create for you. And memorise as many of the Bible verses as you can!

Sinclair B. Ferguson

God is our Creator

Questions
1 - 8

1

Question

Who are you?

Answer

I am

_____.

(Write your name here if this is your book)

No-one else in the whole world is exactly like you. Even twins who look almost the same are different from each other.
Yet God knows each of us. God knows us better than we know each other. He knows us better than we know ourselves. And God loves us. Isn't that amazing?

Memory **V**erse

I will praise you because I am fearfully and wonderfully made.

Psalm 139, verse 14

ACTIVITIES

READING TIME

Read the story in Genesis 2 of how God made us in the very beginning.

TALKING TIME

Think about some of the things which make you **you**: the colour of your eyes, the way you smile. These are all parts of you which God has created. Sometimes we don't like the way we look; there are things we'd like to change. It always helps us to remember that God has a special purpose for each of us. We need to thank him for making us just as we are. God made us and knows us. Maybe there are some things that we hope God doesn't know about. Think about the fact that God knows all about us. Does that make any difference to the way you live?

ACTION TIME

Look at yourself in the mirror and then draw a picture of yourself. Try to get all the details right, even if there are some you would like to change! Remember there is no-one else in the whole world the same as you. Underneath write the words of the Memory Verse.

PRAYER TIME

Dear God, thank you for making me. Thank you that I am special to you and that you love me. Please help me to remember that you know all about me.
Amen.

Question

Why am I here?

Answer

God gave me life so that I could live for him.

God did not need to make you. You might never have been alive! But God wanted you to have life. When you were tiny, God cared for you. He has been looking after you ever since. He wants you to live for him. God really cares about you.

Memory Verse

You gave me life and showed me kindness.
Job 10, verse 12

ACTIVITIES

 **READING TIME**

In Psalm 23 you can find out about how one man, David, knew God cared for him.

TALKING TIME

You won't remember what it was like when you were very small but mum and dad will. They spent a lot of time looking after you. Ask them to tell you about it.

God has also been caring for you all the time. We can't see him caring for us, but we know he is there watching over us. He cares for you so much because he wants you to live for him.

What can you do to show that you are living for God?

ACTION TIME

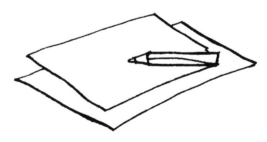

See if you can find some photographs taken when you were a baby. Ask mum or dad to tell you about some of the things that they did to look after you. Write down things you can do that let others know you are living for God. Think about a time when you did something that showed you weren't living for God. Tell God you are sorry.

PRAYER TIME

Dear God, thank you for making me and giving me life. Please help me to live for you. Thank you for caring for me and looking after me. Help me to be caring too. Amen

Question

What is God like?

Answer

God told us what he is like when he said, 'I am who I am'.

One day Moses heard God's voice speaking to him from a burning bush. A fire was burning in the bush, but the bush did not burn up. Moses asked God who he was. God gave him a strange reply.

He said: 'I am who I am'. That means that God had no beginning and no ending. God is like the fire that did not depend on the bush in order to keep burning. He is the one who gives life to everything.

Memory Verse

Before the mountains were born or you brought forth the earth and the world, from everlasting to everlasting you are God.

Psalm 90, verse 2

ACTIVITIES

READING TIME

To learn more of the story of Moses and the burning bush read Exodus 3.

TALKING TIME

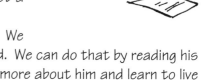

It must have been a great surprise to Moses to hear a bush speak. What kinds of things surprise you?
What do you do if you get a surprise or a fright?
Moses listened to God. We too need to listen to God. We can do that by reading his word so we can find out more about him and learn to live as he wants us to.
How else can you listen to God today?

ACTION TIME

Find out some more about Moses. Make a personal file about him giving details about where he was born, where he was brought up, who his family was, what he did. See Exodus chapters 2 and 3.
Draw a big ear shape and inside it write down or draw all the things which you like to listen to. On the other side of the ear write a message to remind you to listen to good things.

PRAYER TIME

Dear God, thank you for being who you are. Thank you that you give life to everything all around. Thank you for being so great. Help me to listen to you more.
Amen.

Question

Is there only one God?

Answer

There is only one God, and he exists in three persons.

God is different from us. The Bible tells us that there is only one God. But this one God exists in three persons: the Father, the Son and the Holy Spirit. This is a secret which only God himself understands.

But God has told us a little about his secret: he is love. God the Father and the Son and the Spirit love each other. And God wants to share that love with us.

Memory Verse

May the grace of the Lord Jesus Christ, and the love of God, and the fellowship of the Holy Spirit be with you.
2 Corinthians 13, verse 14

ACTIVITIES

READING TIME

Read Mark 1, verses 10 - 11 to find out more about God being three persons in one.

TALKING TIME

How do you think God is different from us? Talk about these differences. What does God want to share with us? What is the mystery that only God understands? What is God's secret?

ACTION TIME

Why do you think this symbol was used for God?

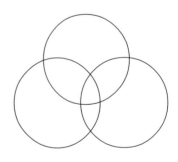

Can you copy it without lifting your pencil from the page?

PRAYER TIME

Dear Lord, you know how difficult it is for me to understand some of your secrets. Please help me to trust you for the things I can't understand.
Amen.

5

Question

Why did God create the world?

Answer

God made the world for his glory and to help us to know, trust and love him.

Are you ever surprised by all the different things God has made?
He made huge elephants and long-necked giraffes.
But God also made small butterflies and thin snowflakes.
He made the sun and the moon and all the stars.
He made the clouds that fly across the sky.
He made you. God is our loving Creator.

Memory Verse

The heavens declare the glory of God; the skies proclaim the work of his hands.
Psalm 19, verse 1.

ACTIVITIES

READING TIME

Psalm 148 talks about all the wonderful things God has made.

TALKING TIME

God made lots of wonderful things in the world. What are your favourites of all God made? Is there anything that God made that you don't really like?
By looking at creation all around us we can learn about God and how wonderful and powerful he is. Every tiny detail is part of his design.

ACTION TIME

Choose the things that you see in the world that help you to love and trust God more. Draw them in a poster. Think of a title for the poster and write it at the top .

PRAYER TIME

Thank you God for all the wonderful things in your world which help me to learn more about your power. Amen.

6

Question

How did God give me life?

Answer

God gave me life through my father and mother.

God made us to live in families where we can be loved. In families we can also learn to love each other.
God gives children to mums and dads so that they can share their love. God the great Creator gives people a part to play in his work. God is kind and generous.

Memory Verse

God sets the lonely in families. Psalm 68, verse 6.

ACTIVITIES

READING TIME

Read Luke 1, verses 57-58 to discover how some people felt at the birth of a child.

TALKING TIME

Who belongs to your family? What are the good things about being part of a family? Families are places where love can be shared. How can you try to share love with others in your family? Can you think of any families that are mentioned in the Bible?

ACTION TIME

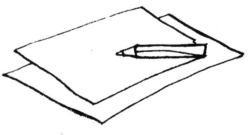

Make a family tree for three Bible families who were sad because they didn't have any children but God turned their sadness to joy by giving them children. (Judges 13; 1 Samuel 1; Luke 1:5-25; 57-80.)

PRAYER TIME

Thank you God for giving me life. Thank you God for putting me in a family. Thank you for the love we can share with each other. Please be close to those who have no family and are feeling lonely. Amen.

ACTIVITIES

Question

Has God always made people in the same way?

Answer

God made the first man, Adam, and the first woman, Eve, in special ways, to show that he alone is our Creator.

The Bible tells us that God made the first man from the ground. His name was Adam. The first woman was made from the first man. Her name was Eve. He made them in special ways to show that they were created by him alone.

The whole human family comes from them — including you!

Memory Verse

And the Lord God formed man from the dust of the ground, and breathed into his nostrils the breath of life.
Genesis 2, verse 7.

READING TIME

Read Genesis 2, verse 7 and verses 20b-23 to find out how God made the first people.

TALKING TIME

In what ways were Adam and Eve special? Why did God make them special? No-one else has ever managed to make a human being in the way that God did.

What sort of things have you created? How did you make them? How was God's creation different from what you make?

ACTION TIME

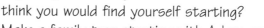

Try to make up your family tree.
If you could trace the tree right back to the beginning where do you think you would find yourself starting?
Make a family tree starting with Adam and Eve, see if you can find out who their children were. (Genesis 4:1-2; see also Luke 3:21-38.)

PRAYER TIME

Lord God you are so wise and wonderful. Help me to praise you as I should. I can't always understand the way you do things but help me to trust you. Amen.

Question

What was the world like after God made it?

Answer

God took time to make the world and filled it with beautiful things.

The Bible tells us that at first the earth was a dark place. But God filled the darkness with light. The earth was also an empty place. God filled the emptiness with plants, trees, fishes, birds and all the animals. Everything God made was perfect. He made Adam to look after his world.

Then he made Eve so that Adam could have a friend. Everything God created was good.

Memory Verse

God saw all that he had made, and it was very good.
       Genesis 1, verse 31.

ACTIVITIES

READING TIME

Read the other parts of the Creation story in Genesis 1.

TALKING TIME

What does it mean if something is perfect? Do you have anything that is perfect? The world God had created was perfect. Who was going to look after this world? Have you ever had to look after anything for anyone? How does it make you feel if you have to be responsible for something?

ACTION TIME

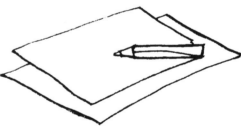

Can you remember the order of things in creation? Write down the seven days of the week and then opposite them write what happened on that day. Try to do it without looking at a Bible. Once you've finished check up with Genesis 1 and fill in anything you missed out.

PRAYER TIME

Thank you, dear Lord, for making so many good things. Help me to look after them for you. Amen.

How things went wrong

Questions
9 - 12

9

Question

Has the world changed since God made it?

Answer

The world God made has been spoiled by sin.

God wanted Adam and Eve to look after and to enjoy his world, and to love him. He told them they could have the fruit from every tree, except one. God wanted them to show him they would obey him just because he is God. Instead, Adam and Eve disobeyed God and sinned. They were no longer friends with God. As a result the whole world was spoiled.

Memory Verse

Sin entered the world through one man, and death through sin.
Romans 5, verse 12.

ACTIVITIES

Look up Genesis 3 and read verses 1 - 13 to find out how God's world was spoiled by sin.

TALKING TIME

Think of somewhere really beautiful that you have been to. Try to imagine going back there and arriving right at the entrance only to be told that you could not go in, and that you could NEVER go in again. How would you feel? That is what it would have been like for Adam and Eve in the garden. Have you ever fallen out with your best friend? How did you feel?

ACTION TIME

Make a list of all the words that you can think of that mean beautiful or could be used to describe the world before sin came.

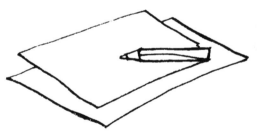

PRAYER TIME

Dear God, it makes me sad to think of your wonderful world being spoiled. Please help me to be more obedient to you. Amen.

10

Question

What is sin?

Answer

Sin is thinking, wanting, or doing what displeases God.

God made us to trust, love and obey him. But when we stop trusting him, we stop loving him. And when we stop loving him, we stop obeying him. We no longer love what he loves. We want to please ourselves. Our hearts become ugly. We all do things that displease God.

We are all sinful.

Memory Verse

Everyone who sins breaks the law; in fact sin is lawlessness. 1 John 3, verse 4.

ACTIVITIES

READING TIME

1 John 5, verses 16-20 tells us more about what displeases God.

TALKING TIME

What sorts of things do you do which displease God and make him sad? What happens when you do them? Do you tell him you are sorry? What do you say?

ACTION TIME

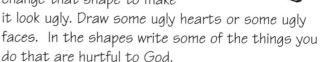

Think of a heart shape and then think of how you could change that shape to make it look ugly. Draw some ugly hearts or some ugly faces. In the shapes write some of the things you do that are hurtful to God.

PRAYER TIME

Dear God, please help me not to do things that really hurt you and other people. Help me to want to please you more in all I think, say and do. Amen.

18

Question

What happens to us because of sin?

Answer

We spoil the world and we lose our friendship with God.

The world is full of sin. Sin leads to suffering and sorrow. We hurt other people and we spoil the world God made.

We die.

God cannot love sin. Worst of all, our sin makes us God's enemies.

Memory Verse

For the wages of sin is death.
Romans 6, verse 23

ACTIVITIES

READING TIME

Read Isaiah 59, verse 2 to discover what happens because of our sin.

TALKING TIME

How is the world spoiled because of sin? What suffering and sorrow can you think of in the world just now? What is an enemy? Do you have any enemies? Is that good? What could you do about it? How can we be enemies of God?

ACTION TIME

How do you feel if someone you know is hurt or something you have made is broken or spoiled? Is there anything you can do about the suffering and sadness that is in the world? Think about poorer parts of the world, our own country and also your own area. Write down what **you** can do to help.

PRAYER TIME

Dear Lord please forgive me for my part in the suffering of the world. Please forgive me and show me what I can do to help.
Amen.

Question

What does our sin deserve?

Answer

Our sin deserves to be punished by God.

God is pure and nothing sinful can live in his presence. We know that when we do wrong we deserve to be punished. Because they had sinned, God sent Adam and Eve away from his presence. Because we have sinned we cannot enter God's presence as we are.

Memory **V**erse

If you, O Lord, kept a record of sins, O Lord, who could stand? Psalm 130, verse 4.

ACTIVITIES

READING TIME

In Psalm 51 you can read about how David felt after he had sinned.

TALKING TIME

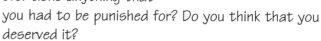

What does it mean to be punished? Who needs punishment? Have you ever done anything that you had to be punished for? Do you think that you deserved it?
Why can't God stand our sin? What would it be like to be sent away from God's presence?

ACTION TIME

There are stories in the Bible of people who have been punished for their sin. Can you think of any and find out where they are found in the Bible? (Joshua 7; Daniel 5; Acts 12:19-24.)

PRAYER TIME

Dear God, you are so pure and holy you can't stand our sin. Please forgive me for my sins.
Amen.

God had a plan

Questions
13 - 16

Question

Why did God not destroy the world sin had spoiled?

Answer

God still loved and looked after the world he had made and had already planned a way of saving us.

We love everyone in our family. We also love other people who like us. But God loved those who turned his back on him.

Each day he watches over and cares for the world. He is working out his plan. He does this because of his love for us.

God's love is really amazing!

Memory Verse

The Lord is good to all; he has compassion on all he has made.
Psalm 145, verse 9.

ACTIVITIES

READING TIME

You can read about how the world was nearly destroyed in Genesis 6 and 7.

TALKING TIME

Can you really imagine loving and wanting to care for someone who is always in trouble and that no-one likes? It would be very hard.
It's much easier to love nice people. How could you show love to someone you find hard to love? What sort of things can you do to show love to people? How are you aware of God's love and care each day?

ACTION TIME

Draw a big heart shape. Inside the shape, draw people or write the names of people you love. Include some people you need to ask God to help you to love.

In another heart write down things you can do to show love. Make a poster showing the world and write the memory verse underneath.

PRAYER TIME

Dear God, thank you for all your love and care over me. I'm so glad that you love me. Please help me to love you more and to be kind and loving to other people.
Amen.

14

Question

What was God's plan to save us?

Answer

God planned to send his Son to die for our sins and to send his Holy Spirit to help us to become like him.

We are not able to save ourselves. Every one of us deserves to be punished for our sins. Only someone who does not deserve to be punished can be punished in our place. God the Father planned that Jesus, his Son, would take our punishment. In the Old Testament we learn how God promised he would do all this. God had a marvellous plan!

Memory Verse

Christ died for sins once for all, the righteous for the unrighteous, to bring you to God.
1 Peter 3, verse 18.

ACTIVITIES

READING TIME

Read the story in Luke 19, verses 1-10 about Zacchaeus and how he discovered God's plan.

TALKING TIME

Were there things in the life of Zacchaeus from which Jesus saved him?
What were they?
Can you find three other people in the Gospels to whom Jesus brought salvation?

ACTION TIME

Can you think of any Bible stories which involved a rescue? (See Exodus 3; Daniel 3 and 6; Acts 12:1-19.) Draw a series of cartoon pictures to describe what happened in one of these passages.

PRAYER TIME

Thank you God that you had a plan to save the world. Thank you Jesus for taking our punishment for us even although we deserved to be punished.
Amen.

15 Question

How did God prepare the way for the Saviour?

Answer

God taught his people about the coming Saviour by sending them prophets, priests and kings.

God sent prophets to speak about the Saviour who would come. The priests offered sacrifices for the sins of the people. The kings ruled to help the people serve God. They all pointed forward to the Saviour who would come. God's special plan was that he was going to send his Son.

Memory Verse

In the past God spoke to our forefathers through the prophets at many times and in various ways, but in these last days he has spoken to us by his Son.

Hebrews 1, verses 1-2.

ACTIVITIES

READING TIME

Read Matthew 3, verses 1-3 to discover how God prepared the way for the Saviour.

TALKING TIME

What does it mean to prepare for something?   What sort of things do you prepare for? Why is it important to prepare?
How could prophets, priests and kings help in God's preparations?
What was the Saviour going to do when he did come?

ACTION TIME

Make up three lists: give them the headings, Prophets, Priests, Kings. Can you find in the Bible three for each list? Why were prophets, priests and kings not needed after Jesus came?

PRAYER TIME

Dear God thank you for teaching us about Jesus. Thank you for your Word the Bible and that we can read it today.
Amen.

16

Question

Who is the Saviour God promised?

Answer

Jesus of Nazareth, God's Son, is the Saviour God promised to send.

Jesus was the Son of God; he called God, 'My Father'. All the promises about the coming Saviour were about him. He was God, but he also became a man in order to take our place.

Long before Jesus was born God promised that he would come. The Old Testament tells us about all these wonderful promises.

Memory Verse

And beginning with Moses and all the prophets, Jesus explained to them what was said in all the Scriptures concerning himself.
Luke 24, verse 27.

ACTIVITIES

Read Psalm 145, verses 13-21 which show that God always keeps his promises.

TALKING TIME

Why was Jesus known as Jesus of Nazareth? If our names were like that nowadays what would you be known as?
What is a Saviour?
Why do we need a Saviour?
What does Jesus have the power to do?

ACTION TIME

Make a scroll like those the Old Testament would have been written on. Write on it all the titles of Jesus that you can find. Isaiah 9, verse 6 might be a good place to start.

PRAYER TIME

Thank you God for Jesus. Thank you for sending a Saviour to us. Thank you for the power Jesus has. Amen.

Jesus came to save

Questions
17-27

17

Question

How did Jesus come into the world?

Answer

Jesus was born in the same way we are, but he was also God's eternal Son.

Mary was Jesus' mother, but he had no human father. That is why the Bible says that Mary was a virgin. Jesus was a small, helpless baby and had to grow. But, unlike you, he did not start to exist just a few months before he was born. He was always God's Son.

Memory **V**erse

All this took place to fulfil what the Lord had said through the prophet Isaiah: 'The virgin will be with child and will give birth to a son, and they will call him Immanuel – which means, "God with us".'

Matthew 1, verse 22.

ACTIVITIES

 To find out about Jesus' mother, Mary, read Luke 1, verses 26-38.

TALKING TIME

People get excited when a new baby is expected. Do you know of anyone with a new baby? How do you think Mary might have felt? How was her baby going to be different from all other babies ever born? Mary must have had a lot of faith and trust in God to help her at this time. Why would it have been hard for her? Think about this very special baby. What can you remember about his birth?

ACTION TIME

Parents usually choose the name for their baby. Mary did not need to choose a name for her baby. Look at Matthew 1, verse 21 to find out how the name was chosen. Can you find out the meaning of your own name? Try to find out if your name was chosen for any special reason.

PRAYER TIME

Dear God, thank you for sending Jesus into the world as a tiny baby. Thank you that he was your own Son. Please help me to understand what this miracle means. Amen.

Question

What was Jesus like when he was young?

Answer

Jesus loved, trusted and obeyed his Heavenly Father every day.

As Jesus grew up, he loved and obeyed God's Word. He learned from the Old Testament what God is like and how to live for him. He read about what he had to do in order to be our Saviour.

Jesus obeyed all of God's commandments. Jesus knew God and loved to be with him. He enjoyed doing what his Heavenly Father said.

Memory Verse

And the child [Jesus] grew and became strong; he was filled with wisdom, and the grace of God was upon him.
    Luke 2, verse 40.

ACTIVITIES

READING TIME

In Luke 2, verses 41-52 you can read about something Jesus did when he was young.

TALKING TIME

In the Bible we are told that Jesus was obedient. Do you know what it means to be obedient? Sometimes it is hard to be obedient but it is something we must learn to do.
Can you think of a time when you have been disobedient? Have you said sorry to God and to the person you were disobedient to?
Jesus liked to spend time with God. Even though you are young do you like to spend time with God?

ACTION TIME

Many people in the Bible obeyed God. Some did not find it easy. Look up these verses to find out about obeying God:
Genesis 6, verse 22;
Jonah 1, verse 3;
Ephesians 6, verse 1.

Can you find other people in the Bible who obeyed God?

PRAYER TIME

Dear Lord, please help me to obey you. You know that sometimes I find it hard. I'm sorry for the times that I am disobedient.
Amen.

Question

What happened when Jesus grew up?

Answer

When Jesus was thirty years old the Holy Spirit came on his life in a special way.

God sent John the Baptist to prepare the way for Jesus.
Jesus was baptised by John in the River Jordan. This was a sign that he had come to take away the sin of the world. Then God's Spirit came in a special way on Jesus and he began to teach that God's kingdom had come. He told all the people to trust and follow him.

Memory Verse

John . . . said, 'Look, the Lamb of God who takes away the sin of the world!'
John 1, verse 29

ACTIVITIES

READING TIME

Read Luke 3, verses 1-22 to find out more about Jesus when he grew up.

TALKING TIME

What would you like to do when you grow up? Why would you like to do what you've chosen?
Jesus' job was to tell people about God and how they could live to please him.
What had John the Baptist's job been?
How can we tell people about Jesus?

ACTION TIME

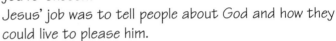

Some people go to other countries to tell people about Jesus. They are called missionaries. Do you know any missionaries? If you do you could write to them or find out more about their work.
You can be a missionary too by telling people about Jesus. Is there someone you know that you could invite to church or Sunday School?

PRAYER TIME

Dear Lord, help me to tell others about Jesus. Be very near to the missionaries who have gone to other countries to tell boys and girls there about Jesus.
Amen.

Question

How did Jesus show that God's kingdom had begun?

Answer

Jesus overcame the temptations of the devil and did many miracles to show that God's kingdom had begun.

The devil tried to stop Jesus from becoming our Saviour.
He tried to get Jesus to sin, but Jesus refused.
Jesus healed sick, lame and blind people.
He rescued people from the power of demons.
Jesus even stilled a storm and gave life to people who had died.
Jesus proved that he was the King!

Memory Verse

Jesus said: Report to John what you have seen and heard: The blind receive sight, the lame walk, those who have leprosy are cured, the deaf hear, the dead are raised, and the good news is preached to the poor.
Luke 7, verse 22.

ACTIVITIES

READING TIME

Read Matthew 4, verses 1-11 to find out about the temptations Jesus faced.

TALKING TIME

What do you think temptation means? What sort of things are you tempted to do? How can you stop yourself from giving in to temptation?
Talk about the temptations Jesus faced.
Jesus was able to do miracles because he had special power from God. Can you remember some of Jesus' miracles? How many can you remember?

ACTION TIME

Draw some pictures of children being tempted to do things. Give them speech bubbles to say what they are going to do, to show that they are not giving in. For example, someone finds some money which does not belong to them. What should they do with it?

PRAYER TIME

Dear Lord, thank you that you are with me when I am tempted. Please help me not to give in to temptation, and help me to do what is right.
Amen.

Question

What was the most important thing that Jesus came to do?

Answer

The most important thing that Jesus came to do was to die for us.

The prophet Isaiah said that God would send a Suffering Servant.
The Servant would die for our sins.
Jesus knew that he was the Suffering Servant promised by God.
He came to take away our sins.
That is why he died on the cross.
He died in order to give us eternal life.

Memory Verse

Christ Jesus came into the world to save sinners.
1 Timothy 1, verse 15

ACTIVITIES

READING TIME

Read Isaiah 53, verses 1-6 and Matthew 8, verse 17 where it tells you about what Jesus came to do.

TALKING TIME

Have you ever done anything really important? Have you been brave, met someone famous, or won a special prize? We all like to be important and feel special.
What was the most important thing Jesus was to do?
What does Jesus' death mean we can now have?

ACTION TIME

Look up these verses: Romans 5, verses 6-9. Copy out verse 8. Put the word die or died in a different colour to remind you what Jesus did for you.
Find out more about being a servant.
Write down what a servant might do.
How was Jesus like a servant?

PRAYER TIME

Dear God, thank you so much for sending Jesus to die for me. Thank you that you can take away our sins. Amen.

Question

How does Jesus save us?

Answer

Jesus lived a perfect life and died on the cross for our sins.

In the Old Testament God accepted the death of a perfect animal as a sacrifice for sins.
But only a perfect man could ever be a true sacrifice for human sin. Jesus was a perfect man and kept all of God's laws. He had no sins and did not deserve to be punished. God accepted the death of Jesus as a sacrifice for our sins. Jesus died for us.

Memory Verse

Christ died for our sins according to the Scriptures.
        1 Corinthians 15, verse 3.

ACTIVITIES

READING TIME

Read John 3, verse 17 to find out how God would save us.

TALKING TIME

What does it mean to be perfect? Are you ever perfect? Jesus was perfect, he never did anything bad at all.
What does the word 'sacrifice' mean?
Why do we not need to sacrifice animals today?

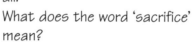

ACTION TIME

Do you know of anyone apart from Jesus who gave their life up to save someone else?
Can you make up a word picture like this for the word Cross?

        Jesu**S**
          c**A**me to
           sa**V**e us through
         his lov**E** for us
         and by **D**ying for us

PRAYER TIME

Dear God, thank you for loving us so much and for sending your Son to be our Saviour.
Amen.

Question

Is Jesus still dead?

Answer

On the Sunday after Jesus died, God raised him to life.

God accepted Jesus' perfect sacrifice for our sins.
Death could no longer keep Jesus in its power.
Jesus died on a Friday afternoon. His spirit went to be with his Father, but his body was placed in a tomb. Early on the Sunday morning God raised Jesus from the dead and gave him new life. Jesus came back to his disciples. For forty days he taught them about his kingdom.

Memory Verse

Remember Jesus Christ, raised from the dead.
2 Timothy 2, verse 8.

ACTIVITIES

Read John 20, verses 1-7 to find out about Jesus no longer being dead.

TALKING TIME

It can be really sad when someone dies, especially if it is someone special. How do you think Jesus' disciples felt when he died?
Why was Jesus' death unusual? How would the ladies who went to the tomb have felt when they discovered that he wasn't there? Can you remember any more of this Bible story?

ACTION TIME

Make a poster with the words **Jesus is Alive** written on it. Decorate it as brightly as possible and hang the poster up somewhere to remind you that Jesus is alive today.

PRAYER TIME

Thank you Jesus that you rose from the dead. Thank you that you are alive today. Amen.

24

Question

Where is Jesus now?

Answer

Jesus has now returned to heaven to be with his Father.

After his resurrection Jesus visited his disciples. He taught them about his kingdom. He promised that he would send his Holy Spirit to them. Then he went back to heaven.

He is in heaven now, caring and praying for us. But one day he will return and everyone will see him again.

Memory Verse

While he [Jesus] was blessing them, he left them and was taken up into heaven.
Luke 24, verse 51.

ACTIVITIES

READING TIME

Read John 14, verse 1-4 to find out where Jesus told his disciples he was going.

TALKING TIME

How do you think Jesus' disciples would have felt when Jesus told them that he was going away?
What did he promise to give them?
What did Jesus promise would happen in the future that is still to happen?

ACTION TIME

Read Luke 24, verses 50-53 and Acts 1, verses 9-11 to find out how Jesus left the disciples.

Write about it in your own words.

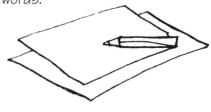

PRAYER TIME

Thank you Jesus that you have gone to prepare a place for me in heaven. Thank you for giving the Holy Spirit to those who trust you.
Amen.

Question

Why did Jesus send the Holy Spirit?

Answer

Jesus sent the Holy Spirit to take his place in our lives.

The Holy Spirit was with Jesus from the beginning of his life. He gave Jesus power to heal the sick. He gave Jesus courage to die on the cross for our sins. He was with Jesus when he rose from the dead. The Spirit was like a best friend.

So when Jesus sent his Spirit it was like sending himself.

Jesus' Spirit now lives in those who trust him.

Memory Verse

Jesus said: I will ask the Father, and he will give you another Counsellor to be with you for ever – the Spirit of truth.

John 14, verses 16-17.

ACTIVITIES

Read Acts 1, verses 6-8 to find out what Jesus said about the Holy Spirit.

TALKING TIME

Do you have a best friend? What do you like to do with that friend? How do you feel when that friend is with you?

How can Jesus be like a best friend to you today? How can you be sure that Jesus is with you? He isn't beside you like a person is, but how is he there?

ACTION TIME

Get some card and cut out a bookmark shape. Write on it:

'Jesus is the Best Friend you can have!'

Decorate it as brightly as you can.

PRAYER TIME

Dear Lord Jesus, thank you that you are the best friend that I can have. Thank you that you are always with me. Amen.

26

Question

Can Jesus be my Saviour?

Answer

Jesus has promised to save all those who trust him.

There is only one way to become a Christian. We must trust in Jesus as our Saviour. We need a Saviour because we are sinful. We cannot save ourselves. We do not deserve Jesus' love and salvation. But he loves us and promises to save everyone who trusts him.
Are you trusting Jesus to be your Saviour?

Memory Verse

'Sirs, what must I do to be saved?' They replied, 'Believe in the Lord Jesus, and you will be saved – you and your house-hold.'
    Acts 16, verses 30-31.

ACTIVITIES

READING TIME

To find out how Jesus can be your Saviour, read John 3, verse 16.

TALKING TIME

Do you know what it means to trust someone? If you are on a high wall and you can't get down maybe some strong adult will tell you to jump and they will catch you. You need to **trust** them that they won't let you fall. Jesus wants us to trust him to take our sins away.

ACTION TIME

Write a letter to a friend about trusting in Jesus. If you want to trust Jesus you will want to spend time reading your Bible and praying every day. Think how you are going to manage to fit this into your day.

PRAYER TIME

Dear Lord Jesus, Thank you that you can be a Saviour to us. Help me to put my trust in you.
Amen.

36

Question

What happens when I trust in Jesus?

Answer

My sins are forgiven and Jesus sends his Spirit into my life.

When we trust in Jesus every one of our sins will be forgiven. When we trust in Jesus he will send his Spirit into our hearts. He sends to us the same Spirit who was with him. Having the Spirit is just like having Jesus in our lives.
The Spirit of Jesus helps us. He makes us more and more like Jesus.

Memory Verse

The Spirit himself testifies with our spirit that we are God's children.
        Romans 8, verse 16.

ACTIVITIES

READING TIME

Read 2 Corinthians 5, verse 17 to find out what happens when you become a Christian.

TALKING TIME

What happens when we trust in Jesus? Who is sent into our hearts? What does the Spirit do for us?

Think of the wind. Can you see the wind? Can you see what the wind does? It's a bit like that with the Spirit. We cannot see the Spirit but we can see what he does by the changes in our lives.

ACTION TIME

Find out what the Spirit does in our lives by reading Galatians 5, verses 22 and 23.
Draw the outline of some fruits. In the middle of each write one of the fruits of the Spirit.
Ask the Holy Spirit to help you show these things in your life.

PRAYER TIME

Dear Lord, thank you for the changes your Spirit makes in my life. Help me to show these changes every day. Amen.

We become like Jesus

Questions
28 - 37

28

Question

Where does Jesus teach us what Christians are like?

Answer

Jesus teaches us what Christians are like in the Beatitudes.

A 'Beatitude' is a saying that tells us how God blesses us, or shows us his love for us.
The Beatitudes are sayings in which Jesus describes Christians. You will find them in Matthew's Gospel, chapter five, verses three to ten. There are eight Beatitudes. Each Beatitude gives us a promise.
Each Beatitude tells us one way in which Jesus will show his love to us.

Memory Verse

I want to know Christ . . . becoming like him.
Philippians 3, verse 10.

ACTIVITIES

READING TIME

Read the Beatitudes in Matthew 5, verses 3-10

TALKING TIME

Whom do you want to be like? A football star? Someone from TV? Someone famous? The person Christians most want to be like is Jesus.

Why do you think that is? What things do you do that show you are like Jesus? Are there things that show you are not like him? In what ways does Jesus want to change them?

ACTION TIME

Think of some of the parts of your body: your eyes, your ears, your mouth, your feet, your hands. How can you use each of these to be more like Jesus?
Draw a person with bubbles coming from different parts of the body and write how each part could be used for God.

PRAYER TIME

Dear God, thank you for the example of Jesus that you have given us to follow. Please help me to be more like Jesus in all I think, say and do.
Amen.

Question

What is the first Beatitude?

Answer

Blessed are the poor in spirit, for theirs is the kingdom of God.

Poor people have no money. They cannot buy what they need.

We are spiritually poor. We cannot buy our salvation.

The poor in spirit are those who know that only Jesus can help them.

Memory Verse

He was rich, yet for your sakes he became poor, so that you through his poverty might become rich.
        2 Corinthians 8, verse 9.

ACTIVITIES

READING TIME

Read Mark 10, verses 17-23 and find out about the rich man.

TALKING TIME

Do you know someone who is really rich? Do they have all the possessions that you could think of? What would you like to do with your money if you were really rich? Do you think that you would be really happy if you were rich? There is something which money cannot buy. What is it?

ACTION TIME

Can you find out what kind of money they used in Bible times? Which Bible stories mention money? (Matthew 10:9; Mark 12:41; Matthew 20:1-16; 22:15-22.) What can you do to help people who are poor?

PRAYER TIME

Dear God, thank you that you love us whether we are rich or poor. Help me not to think that lots of money would make me truly happy. Amen.

30

Question

What is the second Beatitude?

Answer

Blessed are those who mourn, for they will be comforted.

To mourn means to feel very sad. We mourn when someone we love has died. We mourn too when we lose something we love.

When we love God we feel very sorry when we sin and disappoint him. But if we ask him, he will forgive us. Then we will experience the comfort Jesus promised.

Memory Verse

Blessed is he whose transgressions are forgiven, whose sins are covered.
Psalm 32, verse 1.

ACTIVITIES

READING TIME

Read 1 John 1, verse 9 to find out about our sins being forgiven.

TALKING TIME

What should make us feel most sad ? What can we do about that? What makes God sad? What else makes you feel sad? How can you help someone who is mourning?

ACTION TIME

Draw a sad face and a happy face. Write happy and sad words in them. What would change these sad words into happy ones?

PRAYER TIME

Dear God, I am sorry for the wrong things I do. It makes me sad to disappoint you. Please forgive me, and help me to love you better. Amen.

Question

What is the third Beatitude?

Answer

Blessed are the meek, for they will inherit the earth.

To be meek means to be humble. If we are meek, we will accept God's will even when it is difficult for us.

Jesus was meek. He was always willing to do what his Heavenly Father wanted. One day the whole world will belong to Jesus. He will share it with all those he has made humble like himself.

Memory Verse

Humble yourselves, therefore, under God's mighty hand, that he may lift you up in due time.

1 Peter 5, verse 6.

ACTIVITIES

READING TIME

Read Psalm 37, verse 11 to find out more about meek people.

TALKING TIME

Do you always like to be first, or best or chosen to do something? Are you so keen if the task is difficult or something you do not like to do?
What sorts of things are you not very willing to do?
What does it mean to be humble?

ACTION TIME

Simon Peter found it hard to accept Jesus' way. Make a fact file about what happened to Peter in these passages: Matthew 14:22-33; 16:13-23; 17:1-12; 26:69-75.

PRAYER TIME

Dear God, sometimes it is difficult to accept your will. Please help me to remember that you know best in all circumstances.
Amen.

32

Question

What is the fourth Beatitude?

Answer

Blessed are those who hunger and thirst for righteousness, for they will be filled.

Righteousness means being true and faithful to God. When we are hungry and thirsty we ask for something to eat and drink. To hunger and thirst for righteousness means to want everything we do and say to be true and faithful to God. When we want that, Jesus will help us.

Memory Verse

He has filled the hungry with good things.
Luke 1, verse 53.

ACTIVITIES

READING TIME

Read Matthew 6, verse 33 and see what it says about righteousness.

TALKING TIME

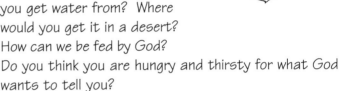

What do you like to eat or drink? Talk about your favourite foods. Where do you get water from? Where would you get it in a desert? How can we be fed by God? Do you think you are hungry and thirsty for what God wants to tell you?

ACTION TIME

Look up Genesis 6, verse 9 and find out who was righteous.
Read James 5, verse 16 to find out what happens when the righteous pray. Draw a desert and show where you would get water.

PRAYER TIME

Dear God, please fill me with more love for you. Help me to want to be true and faithful to you.
Amen.

33

Question

What is the fifth Beatitude?

Answer

Blessed are the merciful, for they will be shown mercy.

To show mercy means to help those who cannot help themselves. Jesus has shown us mercy by taking away our sins.

We show that we have accepted his mercy when we show mercy to others. If we show no mercy to others, we have not yet accepted Jesus' mercy to us. Are you merciful?

Memory Verse

Have mercy on me, O God, according to your unfailing love; according to your great compassion blot out my transgressions.
Psalm 51, verse 1.

ACTIVITIES

READING TIME

Read Matthew 18, verses 21-35 to find out about a harsh servant.

TALKING TIME

Do you know of anyone who needs help? Is there anything that you could do to help them?
What could someone do to help you?
What is the best thing that Jesus has done to help us?

ACTION TIME

Draw or write about three people you know who need help. Write a sentence prayer for each of them.

PRAYER TIME

Dear God, thank you that you have shown us mercy. Help me to show mercy to other people. Amen.

Question

What is the sixth Beatitude?

Answer

Blessed are the pure in heart, for they will see God.

Something that is pure has nothing else mixed with it. Pure water is clean; there is nothing in it except water.
A pure heart is a heart that loves Jesus first.

When we ask Jesus to give us a pure heart he will help us to put away impure things. Then we will be able to love him even more.

Memory Verse

I seek you with all my heart; do not let me stray from your commands.
Psalm 119, verse 10.

ACTIVITIES

READING TIME

Read Philippians 4, verse 8 and find out what things we should think about.

TALKING TIME

Think about the things that you really love and that are very important to you. Have you learned to love Jesus more than any of these things? What sort of things do we need to get rid of so that we can have pure hearts? Are there things that you read or watch on TV that stop your heart from being pure?

ACTION TIME

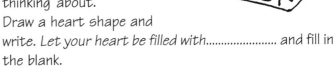

Draw a head shape with a think bubble. Write the things from Philippians 4, verse 8 that we should be thinking about.
Draw a heart shape and write. *Let your heart be filled with.......................* and fill in the blank.

PRAYER TIME

Dear Lord, please help me to have a pure heart. Help me to keep my eyes, ears and mind away from things that are not good for me. Amen.

35

Question

What is the seventh Beatitude?

Answer

Blessed are the peacemakers, for they will be called sons of God.

Jesus, God's Son, came to be a peacemaker. When we trust him, our sins are forgiven. We are at peace with God. God is not our enemy. God's children want to tell others about what Jesus has done. If they trust him, they too will have peace with God. Then we will be peace-makers too!

Memory Verse

Therefore, since we have been justified through faith, we have peace with God through our Lord Jesus Christ.

Romans 5, verse 1.

ACTIVITIES

READING TIME

In James 3, verse 17 and 18 you can find out some more about peacemakers.

TALKING TIME

What does peace mean to you? What is the opposite of peace? Can you think of places in the world where there is no peace today? Do you know of people in these places who are trying to be peacemakers? How can true lasting peace be found? Could you be a peacemaker at school?

ACTION TIME

There is a symbol which is often associated with peace today. Can you find out what it is? Why is it used? How many other words indicating peace can you write down? Can you think of ways in which you can be a peacemaker?

PRAYER TIME

Dear God, thank you that true and lasting peace can be found in you. Help me to help others find peace with you too. Amen.

36

Question

What is the eighth Beatitude?

Answer

Blessed are those who are persecuted because of righteousness, for theirs is the kingdom of heaven.

Jesus lived for God and taught about him. Some people hated him and tried to hurt or persecute him. When we belong to Jesus we will live for him and speak about him. Sometimes even our friends will not like us because we love Jesus. They will say and do things which hurt us. But Jesus will be with us. He will help us.

Memory Verse

Paul and Barnabas said: 'We must go through many hardships to enter the kingdom of God.'

Acts 14, verse 22.

ACTIVITIES

READING TIME

Read Matthew 13, verses 18-23 to find out what is said about persecution.

TALKING TIME

What does the word 'persecution' mean?
Have you ever been persecuted or known someone who has been?
What can you do if you or a friend are being persecuted?
Who is with us even in these hard situations?

ACTION TIME

Paul was often persecuted. Can you make a criminal record card for him using these Bible references to help you? Acts 9:20-25; 14:8-20; 16:16-40; 17:1-15; 19:23-41; 21:27-36; 24:5-21; 25:6-12; 26:1-32.
Would you really stamp it guilty? Can you find out where Christians are persecuted today because of their faith?

PRAYER TIME

Dear Lord, thank you that you understand about people not liking us because we believe in you. Please help me to go on loving them. Be near Christians who are being persecuted. Amen.

Question

How can I become more like Jesus?

Answer

God helps me to become more like Jesus by giving me his Holy Spirit.

Jesus gives us a new heart to love and trust him. Jesus also sends his Holy Spirit into our hearts. The Holy Spirit was always with Jesus. The Holy Spirit knows how to make us more like Jesus. He helps us to know and to do what pleases God.

Memory Verse

We who . . . reflect the Lord's glory, are being transformed into his likeness.
          2 Corinthians 3, verse 18.

ACTIVITIES

Read Ezekiel 36, verses 25-27 to find out what it means to have a new heart.

TALKING TIME

What does it mean to be given a new heart?
What does it mean to have the Holy Spirit in your life?
How can the Holy Spirit help us?

ACTION TIME

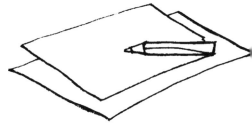

Look back at all the Beatitudes and choose the one that is special to you or that you want to remember. Write it on a poster. Or you could write all of them out and try to learn them.

PRAYER TIME

Thank you God for sending your Spirit. Help me to become more like Jesus every day.
Amen.

We obey God

Questions
38 - 50

Question

How can I discover what pleases God?

Answer

God tells me what pleases him in his Word, the Bible.

The Bible was written by many different people, like Moses and David, Peter and Paul. The Holy Spirit guided them to write exactly what God wanted. In the Bible, the Old Testament tells us how God prepared the way to send Jesus. The New Testament tells us about Jesus and teaches us how to live for him. Throughout the Bible God teaches us what pleases him.

Memory Verse

Your word is a lamp to my feet and a light for my path.
Psalm 119, verse 105.

ACTIVITIES

READING TIME

Look up Psalm 12, verse 6 to find out what God's word is compared to.

TALKING TIME

Do you have a favourite book? Why do you like it? Can you think of a book which is very useful? What can you use it for?
The Bible is the best book of all. Which parts of the Bible do you like best? Why? Whom can you think of who wrote things down in the Bible? How did they know what to write?

ACTION TIME

Get your Bible out and have a good look at it. Look at the list of all the books near the beginning. Can you learn the order of the books off by heart?
How many books are in the Old Testament and how many are in the New Testament?
How many books are there in the whole Bible?

PRAYER TIME

Dear God, thank you for giving us the Bible. Help me to realize how important and wonderful it is. Help me to understand it better when I read it. Help me to find out what pleases you and help me to live like that. Amen.

Question

Where does God teach us what pleases him?

Answer

God teaches us what pleases him in the Ten Commandments.

God's people were slaves in Egypt at one time. God rescued them and promised to take them to a new country. He told them what to do to please him. He gave them ten special commands to obey.
You can find these commands in Exodus chapter twenty. Jesus wants you to keep them.

Memory **V**erse

I run in the path of your commands, for you have set my heart free.
Psalm 119, verse 32.

ACTIVITIES

Read Exodus 3, verses 7-10 to find out about the slaves in Egypt.

TALKING TIME

What is a slave? What would it be like to be a slave? What rules do you have to obey in your home, at school or when playing sport? Why do we need rules? Do you always keep them?

ACTION TIME

Look up Exodus chapter 19 and draw a poster of what it describes.
Get ready to start a fact sheet on life in Egypt and the journey the people took. Add a bit to it every day.

PRAYER TIME

Thank you God for the ten commandments. As I learn about them help me to want to keep them.
Amen.

40

Question

Why do the Ten Commandments tells us what we are not to do?

Answer

The Ten Commandments tells us what we are not to do because God wants us to avoid spoiling our lives.

Has anyone ever said to you: 'Don't ever do that'?
You must not touch fire, because it burns. You must not play with the electric socket, because it can be dangerous. You need to avoid these things if you want to be safe and well.
God speaks to us like that.
God says: 'Do not do these things; they will harm you.'
God knows best; we should listen to what he says.

Memory Verse

I will never forget your precepts, for by them you have preserved my life.

Psalm 119, verse 93.

ACTIVITIES

READING
TIME

Read John 14, verse 21 to find out something else about keeping the commands.

TALKING TIME

What things have you been told not to do because they might harm you?
Have you ever been hurt because you have done something you were told not to do?
How did you feel?
Why do you think we need rules?

ACTION TIME

Make up some warning signs like traffic signs to remind yourself of things not to do. Think of things that the Bible talks about.

Find out in Exodus chapter 1 about what the slaves had to do in Egypt and write or draw about it for your factsheet.
Find out who first received the ten commands and how they were given.

PRAYER TIME

Thank you God that you want to protect us from spoiling our lives. Thank you for caring so much about us.
Amen.

Question

What is the first commandment?

Answer

You shall have no other gods before me.

We belong to God. He gave us life so that we would trust, love and serve him. Jesus died so that we would belong to him and live for him. That is why Jesus must always have the first place in our lives. When we put him first we will want to live in his way.

Have you put Jesus first?

Memory Verse

Jesus died for all, that those who live should no longer live for themselves but for him who died for them and was raised again.
2 Corinthians 5, verse 15.

ACTIVITIES

READING TIME

Read Psalm 81, verses 8-10

TALKING TIME

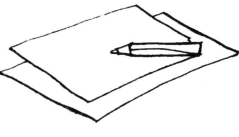

What does it mean to you to have a god other than God? Can you think of things that some people have as their gods? Who comes first in your life? What does it mean to belong to God? Do you belong to God?

ACTION TIME

Start to write out the commands each day as you read them.
In your factsheet add something you know about Moses.

PRAYER TIME

Dear God please help me to belong to you and not to have anything in my life that is more important than you.
Amen.

42

Question

What is the second commandment?

Answer

You shall not make for yourself an idol.

An idol is a false god. People sometimes made models of their false gods and bowed down to them. We sometimes have idols too. An idol is a person or a thing we think about and love more than we love Jesus. If we love Jesus we will not want to have idols in our hearts.

Memory Verse

They tell how you turned to God from idols to serve the living and true God.
1 Thessalonians 1, verse 9.

ACTIVITIES

READING TIME

Read 1 John 5, verse 21 to find out what John says about idols.

TALKING TIME

Can you think of anything that could be an idol in your life or home? Can you do anything about it?
How can you sometimes have an idol and not realize it?
Sometimes in the Bible we read of idols being smashed. Can you find out where? (Exodus 23:23-27; Deuteronomy 9:7-21; 2 Kings 18:4.)

ACTION TIME

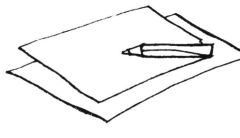

Write down the next command on your list.
Look up Exodus 14 and in your factsheet write about or draw how the people crossed the Red Sea and how they must have felt.

PRAYER TIME

Thank you God that you can help us to get rid of idols. Please come to people who worship idols and help them to find out about you.
Amen.

Question

What is the third commandment?

Answer

You shall not misuse the name of the Lord your God.

When we love someone their name is important to us. Their name tells us who they are. We say their name with love. God's name is special to us because he is God, and because we love him.
Whenever we use his name we must do so with love. If we love him we will love and praise his name.

Memory Verse

Glorify the Lord with me; let us exalt his name together.
            Psalm 34, verse 3.

ACTIVITIES

READING TIME

Philippians 2, verse 10 tells us how important God's name is.

TALKING TIME

Whom do you love? Do you like it when someone says something horrible about that person? Do you ever hear people using God's name in a bad way? How does that make you feel? Why must we not use God's name wrongly?

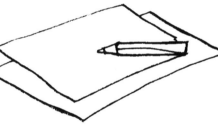

ACTION TIME

Add this command to your list.
For your factsheet find out and write or draw about how the people lived in the wilderness. (Exodus 16, 17.) Can you find out in the Bible some of the different names God is known by?

PRAYER TIME

Dear God, I praise you that your name is so special. Please help me to use it lovingly.
Amen.

44

Question

What is the fourth commandment?

Answer

Remember the Sabbath day by keeping it holy.

God spent six of his days to make the world. On the seventh day he stopped to enjoy it. Like God, we are to do all our work in six days each week. On the seventh day we can rest and admire what he has done. Jesus rose from the dead and met with the disciples on the first day of the week.

That is why Christians begin the week with the day of rest.

Memory Verse

And God blessed the seventh day and made it holy, because in it he rested from the work of creating that he had done.
Genesis 2, verse 3.

ACTIVITIES

READING TIME

Read Exodus 16, verse 23 and 31, verses 12-17 to find out more about the Sabbath.

TALKING TIME

What do you think it means to keep a day holy? What sort of things can you do on Sunday to make it special? How can we especially meet with Jesus on a Sunday? Why is our special day now the first day of the week?

ACTION TIME

Write or draw what you can do on Sunday to keep it special.
Add the fourth command to your list.
On your factsheet write down the places the people travelled through after leaving Egypt or copy a map from your Bible. (Exodus 12:13–19:2.)

PRAYER TIME

Dear God, please help me to remember about your day and try to keep it special. Be with those who cannot join us to worship you on Sunday.
Amen.

Question

What is the fifth commandment?

Answer

Honour your father and your mother.

God gave us fathers and mothers to love and care for us. Best of all, they can tell us about Jesus and his love for us. They can tell us everything God has taught them. God wants us to love them and do what they say. He wants us to do this because we love him. Jesus did that. Will you be like him?

Memory Verse

Then Jesus went down to Nazareth with Mary and Joseph and was obedient to them.

Luke 2, verse 51.

ACTIVITIES

READING TIME

Read Ephesians 6, verses 1-3.

TALKING TIME

What does it mean to honour someone? In what ways do fathers and mothers care for us?
How can you show that you love them?
Ask your parents to tell you something of what God has taught them.

ACTION TIME

Make a poster and in your own words write out the fifth commandment.
For your factsheet find out what kind of food was eaten by the Israelites when they were in the desert. (Exodus 16.)

PRAYER TIME

Thank you God for mothers and fathers who take care of us and teach us about you. Amen.

46

Question

What is the sixth commandment?

Answer

You shall not murder.

God wants us to be like him. Like God we are to love and care for everyone he has made. We must not destroy someone else's life.
That would be to destroy what God has made.
Sometimes we try to do that by what we say as well as by what we do.
That, too, is wrong.
God wants us to help others, not to destroy them.

Memory Verse

Love does no harm to its neighbour.
           Romans 13, verse 10.

ACTIVITIES

READING TIME

Read James 3, verses 3-10 to find out how important it is to be careful in what we say.

TALKING TIME

How can we destroy something or someone by what we say?
Have you ever felt hurt by what someone has said?
Is it OK to hate someone?
Is there someone you feel you hate? How can you learn to love them instead?

ACTION TIME

Draw some faces with speech bubbles showing people saying kind things to one another. Add this command to your list.
In your factfile add some details of what the people did while Moses was up on the mountain. (Exodus 32:1-16.)

PRAYER TIME

Dear Lord, please help me to be careful about what I say. Help me to use kind words to other people.
Amen.

Question

What is the seventh commandment?

Answer

You shall not commit adultery.

When a man and a woman marry they promise they will always love each other. To 'commit adultery' means to break that promise. It means to act as though you were married to someone else. To commit adultery is to lie and to cheat. God must hate it; we should too. If you get married, make sure you keep this commandment because you love God.

Memory Verse

Guard yourself in your spirit, and do not break faith.
Malachi 2, verse 16.

ACTIVITIES

READING TIME

Read 1 Corinthians 7, verse 2 where Paul talks about marriage.

TALKING TIME

Find out from your mum or dad about when they got married. Ask them about the promises they made. See if you can look at the photos of their wedding too.
What was given as a symbol of their love?

ACTION TIME

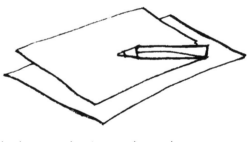

Add the seventh command to your list. In your fact sheet find out about where the ten commands were to be kept and write or draw about it. (Exodus 25:10-22.)

PRAYER TIME

Dear God, thank you for giving us commands for our good. Help me to be true to those I love, always.
Amen.

Question

What is the eighth commandment?

Answer

You shall not steal.

Stealing means taking something that belongs to someone else. Some people steal from shops. But there are other ways of stealing.

You steal when you cheat. You steal if you take pay for work you have not done.
When we steal we cheat God as well. God wants us to share what we have, not to steal what belongs to others.

Memory Verse

He who has been stealing must steal no longer, but must work, doing something useful with his hands, that he may have something to share with those in need.

Ephesians 4, verse 28.

ACTIVITIES

READING TIME

Read Leviticus 6, verses 1-6 to find out what God says about stealing.

TALKING TIME

What does the word stealing mean to you?
What different ways can you steal?
Have you ever taken something which didn't belong to you or even been tempted to?
What is someone who steals called?

ACTION TIME

Work out what you would do if you were tempted to steal or saw someone else stealing.
Add this to your list of commands.
Find out about why the commands had to be given twice and add this to your fact file. (Exodus 32:17-20; 34:1-7, 27-28.)

PRAYER TIME

Dear Lord, please forgive me for when I have given in to the temptation to steal or cheat. Help me to trust you more and to be stronger. Amen.

49

Question

What is the ninth commandment?

Answer

You shall not give false testimony against your neighbour.

God wants everything we say to be true. So we must not tell lies. We must not try to harm people by what we say. Sometimes we say things about others that we know are not true. Sometimes we do not say the things we know are true. That too must be wrong. God wants us to use our tongues to tell others the truth about Jesus.

Memory Verse

The tongue is a small part of the body, but it makes great boasts. Consider what a great forest is set on fire by a small spark.
James 2, verse 5.

ACTIVITIES

READING TIME

Read Psalm 34, verses 11-14 where the psalmist tells us how important it is to watch what we say.

TALKING TIME

Have you ever told lies? Can you remember why and what happened? Did you get found out? Who knows — even if you think no-one has found out? What is the opposite of lies?

ACTION TIME

Add the ninth command to your list.
Make a list of the different ways in which you might be tempted to tell lies. How can you overcome the temptation?

PRAYER TIME

Dear Lord, thank you that you have given me a tongue. Please help me to use it wisely. Amen.

Question

What is the tenth commandment?

Answer

You shall not covet anything that belongs to your neighbour.

God has a special purpose for each one of us. He gives us different things to use for him.
He wants us to be content with what he gives us. To covet means to wish that God had given you what he has given to someone else. It means to be jealous.
If we are thankful for what God has given us we will not covet what he has given to someone else. We will be glad that God shares his gifts with all his people.

Memory Verse

I have learned the secret of being content in any and every situation . . . I can do everything through him who gives me strength.
        Philippians 4, verses 12-13.

ACTIVITIES

READING TIME

Read James 4, verses 1-3 where the writer talks about wanting things you can't have.

TALKING TIME

Can you think of something that belongs to someone else, that you would really like? How do you feel about that person? What can you be thankful to God for that he has given to you? Can you thank him for what he has given to others too?

ACTION TIME

Look up these verses to find out more:
Philippians 4, verse 11,
1 Timothy 6, verse 8
Hebrews 13, verse 5.
What do you find in each verse?
Add this command to your list.
Read Deuteronomy 34, verses 1-4 and add what happened to Moses to your factfile.

PRAYER TIME

Dear Lord, thank you for all you have given to me. Please help me to be glad about what others have. Amen.

How the Bible helps us

Questions
51-54

51

Question

How does God help me to keep his commandments?

Answer

God has given me his Word, his presence, his people and special signs of his love, to help me.

In the Bible, God speaks to us. In prayer, we speak to God. In the church, God's people surround us with his love. Baptism is Jesus' sign that we belong to him. The Lord's Supper is Jesus' sign to show us how much he has loved us.
By giving us these things God helps us to live for him.

Memory **V**erse

His divine power has given us everything we need for life and godliness.
2 Peter 1, verse 3.

ACTIVITIES

Remind yourself of the 10 commandments by looking up Exodus 20, verses 1-17 and John 15, verses 9-14.

TALKING TIME

What things does God give us to help us to keep his rules? Talk about these things. Why do we need help to keep them?

ACTION TIME

Draw an open hand shape and coming from it write the things which God gives us to help us to keep his commands.

PRAYER TIME

Dear God, thank you for your ten rules. It can be so easy to break rules; thank you that you can help us to keep your rules. Please help me.
Amen.

52

Question

What is the most important thing the Bible tells me?

Answer

The most important thing the Bible tells me about is Jesus.

The Bible is God's Word and has two parts, the Old Testament and the New Testament.
The Old Testament contains 39 books telling us how God prepared the way for Jesus to come. God gave his people many promises that he would send them a Saviour.
Many Old Testament people who lived before Jesus trusted God's promise that he would save them through Jesus. Their sins were forgiven because they trusted in the Saviour God promised to send.

Memory **V**erse

'Abraham believed God, and it was credited to him as righteousness'
Romans 4, verse 3.

ACTIVITIES

READING TIME

Read 2 Timothy 3, verses 14-17 to find out more about God's Word.

TALKING TIME

What did Paul tell Timothy about the Bible to help him to understand its message?
What did he say the Bible is useful for?

ACTION TIME

Look at a list of all the books in the Old Testament. How many of them are the names of people?
Choose five of them and write a sentence saying why each of them became famous.

PRAYER TIME

Dear God, thank you for giving me the Bible to tell us all about Jesus. Help me to read and learn from it more. Amen.

Question

Why did God give us the New Testament?

Answer

God has given us the New Testament to tell us all we need to know about Jesus.

The New Testament contains 27 books:
The four Gospels describe Jesus' life, death and resurrection.
The Acts of the Apostles tells us how the message about Jesus spread.
The twenty-one Letters explain what Jesus has done for us and how he changes our lives.
The book of Revelation tells us about the final victory Jesus will win.

Memory Verse

These are written that you may believe that Jesus is the Christ, the Son of God, and that by believing you may have life in his name.
John 20, verse 31.

ACTIVITIES

READING TIME

Read Luke 1, verses 1-4 to find out more about why we have the New Testament.

TALKING TIME

Can you find out what language the New Testament was written in?
Who wrote the New Testament?
How many of the books are names of people or connected to places?

ACTION TIME

Find a map of Bible places and see if you can find the places which have names like some of the New Testament books. Why were the books given names like this?

PRAYER TIME

Dear God, thank you that we have the good news of Jesus in your Word. Help me to share it with others.
Amen.

Question

How can I get to know the Bible?

Answer

I can get to know the Bible by reading it, listening to it being explained in church, and by thinking about what it says.

God has spoken in his Word, the Bible, and he wants us to listen to what he says. It will help you to get to know the Bible if you read a passage from it each day. Then you will learn the message of the whole Bible. In this way you will get to know Jesus better. You will learn everything he wants to teach you. Each time you read the Bible, pray that God will speak to you.

Memory Verse

Jesus answered, 'It is written: "Man does not live on bread alone, but on every word that comes from the mouth of God".'
Matthew 4, verse 4.

ACTIVITIES

READING TIME

Read Matthew 4, verse 4 to see how important it is to read the Bible.

TALKING TIME

Why do you think it is important to read the Bible?
What have you learned recently from reading the Bible? How can you get to know it better?
Sometimes we say that the Bible is like food. In what ways is that true?

ACTION TIME

Write a letter explaining why the Bible is so important.
If you don't already read the Bible every day why not start now?

PRAYER TIME

Dear Lord, help me not to be too busy to read your Word. Help me to take time every day.
Amen.

Learning how to pray

Questions
55 - 64

Question

What is prayer?

Answer

Prayer is talking to God, praising him for his greatness, thanking him for his love, and asking for his help.

We like to talk to people we love. We go to them when we need help. When we love God we talk to him about everything in our lives.
We tell him why we love him so much. We spend time with him. We ask him for help. We enjoy being in his presence in a special way.

Memory Verse

If I had cherished sin in my heart, the Lord would not have listened; but God has surely listened and heard my voice in prayer.
Psalm 66, verses 18-19.

ACTIVITIES

READING TIME

Read Luke 22, verse 41, Matthew 6, verse 9 and Daniel 6, verses 10-11 to see what they say about prayer.

TALKING TIME

Is there someone you enjoy talking to?
When do you talk to them? What do you like to talk to your friends about?
When can we talk to God?
What sort of things can we say to God?
What difference can this make in our lives?

ACTION TIME

When will you pray today?
Keep a little book to write down things to pray about.
Remember to praise and thank God and tell him you are sorry for wrong things you have said and done.
Write down what you will pray about today.

PRAYER TIME

Dear God, thank you that I can talk to you about anything, at any time. Help me to tell you about everything.
Amen.

Question

How can we learn to pray?

Answer

We can use the prayer Jesus taught his disciples as a model.

Jesus taught his disciples this outline for prayer:

Our Father in Heaven,
hallowed be your name,
your kingdom come,
your will be done
on earth as it is in heaven.
Give us this day our daily bread.
Forgive us our debts,
as we have forgiven our debtors.
And lead us not into temptation,
but deliver us from evil.

Memory Verse

One day Jesus was praying in a certain place. When he finished, one of his disciples said to him, 'Lord, teach us to pray, just as John taught his disciples'.
Luke 11, verse 1.

ACTIVITIES

READING TIME

Read Matthew 6, verses 5-14.

TALKING TIME

What does it mean to be a model for something? How can the Lord's Prayer be a model? Look at the verses surrounding the Lord's Prayer in Matthew 6, and find out what else Jesus says about prayer. Why do you think he says these things? Is there anything that you can learn about prayer from the verses which follow?

ACTION TIME

Copy the Lord's Prayer out and put illustrations around it. Try to learn it by heart.

PRAYER TIME

Make up a prayer of your own modelled on the Lord's Prayer or use the Lord's Prayer itself today. Amen.

Question

What do we mean when we pray, 'Hallowed be your name'?

Answer

We pray, 'Hallowed be your name' because we want God to be loved and his name to be special.

'Hallow' is a very old word meaning, 'to make holy'. To make something holy means to keep it special for God. People do not always treat God as special. Sometimes they do not care about God's name at all. Jesus taught us to pray that God's name would be loved all over the world. We can begin by asking him to help us to love his name.

Memory Verse

I will exalt you my God the King; I will praise your name for ever and ever.
        Psalm 145, verse 1.

ACTIVITIES

READING TIME

Read Psalm 30, verse 4 and Psalm 99 and find the word holy.

TALKING TIME

How do some people show that they do not respect God's name?
How can we treat God as special?
How can we keep ourselves holy for God?
Did you know that, 'Amen' at the end of our prayers means, 'Lord, I really do mean this prayer'?

ACTION TIME

Do some research and see if you can find any other prayers in the Bible.

(Nehemiah 9, Daniel 9, John 17.) Find out who was praying and why. Find some pictures from old magazines of people from other countries. Cut them out and make them into a poster. Think of something to write on it about God's name being loved throughout the world.

PRAYER TIME

Dear Lord, thank you that your name is special. Please help me to love your name more and more.
Amen.

Question

Why do we pray 'Your kingdom come, your will be done on earth as it is in heaven'?

Answer

We pray this because we want God's will to be done perfectly and joyfully, just as it is in heaven.

God is King in heaven. There everyone enjoys doing his will. But that is not yet true on earth. Even those who love Jesus do not yet perfectly obey him. We need God's help in order to obey him better. That is why we pray for God's kingdom to come on the earth.

Memory Verse

Seek first his kingdom and his righteousness, and all these things will be given to you as well.
Matthew 6, verse 33.

ACTIVITIES

READING TIME

Read Matthew 7, verses 15-23 to find out what Jesus said about doing God's will.

TALKING TIME

What difference do you think there is between the way God's will is done on earth and in heaven?
Why is it important to obey God? Do we always obey God just now? How can we obey him better?

ACTION TIME

How could you pray more for God's kingdom to come? Are there any missionaries that you know of to whom you can write?

PRAYER TIME

Dear God, thank you that your kingdom will come on earth. Help me to do your will more.
Amen.

Question

Why do we need to pray for 'our daily bread'?

Answer

We pray for our daily bread because we depend on God each day for everything.

God has made us with bodies that need food. Food gives us strength to serve God. The farmer needs the rain and the sun God sends to grow wheat. The baker needs God's strength to turn the wheat flour into bread. We need God's strength to eat the bread! We can do nothing without him. We all depend on God every day of our lives.

Memory Verse

My God will meet all your needs according to his glorious riches in Christ Jesus.

Philippians 4, verse 19.

ACTIVITIES

READING TIME

Read Matthew 6, verses 25-34 to find out more about God providing us with everything we need.

TALKING TIME

What are some of the ways in which you depend on God?
Do you know of any situations where God has provided for someone in a really marvellous way?
How did God provide for the children of Israel after they left Egypt? (Exodus 16, 17.)

ACTION TIME

We buy most of our food from shops, but can you work out where some items originally came from?
Begin by thinking about some of the fruit that we eat.

PRAYER TIME

Dear God, thank you that you provide us with everything that we need. Thank you for the great variety of food that you have given to us.
Amen.

60 Question

Why do we ask God to 'forgive our debts'?

Answer

We ask God to forgive our debts because we cannot pay the cost of the forgiveness of our sins.

A debt is something we owe and must pay back.
God wants us to obey him perfectly, but instead we have sinned. We deserve to be punished. We owe him not only for our lives but for our sins.
We can never pay the debt we owe God. But God has sent Jesus to pay the debt for us.
Now our debt can be cancelled.

Memory Verse

If you, O Lord, kept a record of sins, O Lord, who could stand? But with you there is forgiveness; therefore you are feared.
Psalm 130, verses 3-4.

ACTIVITIES

READING TIME

Read Mark 2, verses 7-10 where Jesus talks about forgiving sin.

TALKING TIME

What does it mean to be in debt? How do people get into debt? Have you ever owed anyone anything? Did you pay them back?
Can we pay God back what we owe him?
What does it mean if something is cancelled?
Could a football game be cancelled or a party?
Why might things get cancelled?
How is our debt to God cancelled?

ACTION TIME

Read the rest of the story in Mark 2 and write the story in your own words or draw a cartoon describing it.

PRAYER TIME

Dear God, thank you that you want to forgive us. Thank you for sending Jesus to pay and cancel our debt. Amen.

Question

Why do we pray to be forgiven 'as we forgive our debtors'?

Answer

We say 'as we forgive our debtors' because if God has forgiven us we should forgive others.

God has forgiven us a debt we could never pay for our sins. Do we forgive others?
If we do not forgive others, our hearts must be very hard. That shows we have not really seen that we need forgiveness. We have not really asked for God's forgiveness. If we have been forgiven we will want to forgive others.

Memory Verse

But if you do not forgive men their sins, your Father will not forgive your sins.
        Matthew 6, verse 15.

ACTIVITIES

READING TIME

In Matthew 18, verses 21-35 Jesus says more about forgiveness.

TALKING TIME

Why should we want to forgive others?
What can we do about this? What does it mean to have a hard heart?
How do we know if our hearts are hard?
Do you think you need to be forgiven? Is there anyone you need to forgive?

ACTION TIME

Draw a cartoon with several pictures showing what happened in Matthew 18, verses 21-35.

PRAYER TIME

Dear God, thank you that you forgive us. Please help me to forgive people when they do something wrong to me. Amen.

Question

Why do we pray 'Lead us not into temptation but deliver us from evil'?

Answer

We pray 'Lead us not into temptation, but deliver us from evil' because we know that we are weak and may give in to temptation.

God gives new hearts to his children. But sin is still left in our lives. We are not yet perfect, as we shall be in heaven. We do not have enough strength of our own to resist temptation. We need God's help all the time. He has promised to protect us.

Memory Verse

God is faithful; he will not let you be tempted beyond what you can bear. But when you are tempted, he will also provide a way out so that you can stand up under it.

1 Corinthians 10, verse 13.

ACTIVITIES

READING TIME

In Luke 4, verses 1-13 you can find out how Jesus overcame temptation.

TALKING TIME

In what three ways was Jesus tempted?
How did he use the Bible for protection?
How can we resist temptation?
How can God's Word the Bible protect us?

ACTION TIME

In Ephesians 6, verses 10-18 you can find out how Paul told people to protect themselves with God's armour.
Draw a soldier wearing the different parts of the armour. Write beside them a description of the Christian's armour against temptation.

PRAYER TIME

Thank you God that you want to protect me from temptation. I need your help; please give it to me. Amen.

Question

How can I be sure that God hears my prayers?

Answer

I can be sure God hears my prayers because he has promised to listen to me when I pray in Jesus' name.

God looks after the whole world. But his children are special to him. He listens carefully when we speak to him. And Jesus has given us an extra promise.
He said: When you pray, use my name. We are to tell our Heavenly Father that we are Jesus' friends. That is another reason why he will listen to us very carefully.

Memory Verse

Jesus said: Until now you have not asked for anything in my name. Ask and you will receive and your joy will be complete.
John 16, verse 24.

ACTIVITIES

READING TIME

In Mark 10, verse 14 Jesus speaks of how special children are to him.

TALKING TIME

How can you be sure that God hears you?
Do you ever feel that God doesn't hear you speaking?
When you feel like that, remind yourself that God has promised to hear you. We are Jesus' special friends.

ACTION TIME

What do you use to listen with? What do you like to listen to? Draw a large ear shape and in it write any other words that mean, 'to listen'.
Make yourself a bookmark with the words, 'God hears my prayers'.

PRAYER TIME

Lord, you have promised to love me and care for me. Thank you that I am safe in your presence.
Amen.

Question

Will God always answer me when I pray?

Answer

God always answers my prayers by giving me what is best for me, for others, and for his own glory.

God knows what is best. Sometimes he gives us what we ask for because that is best. But sometimes he wants us to be patient. He says 'Wait'. He wants us to keep trusting him, and to keep praying. Sometimes God says 'No', because his plan is better than ours. Sometimes we ask for the wrong thing, or for the wrong reasons. But God always hears our prayers, and he always answers them.

Memory Verse

'Father,' Jesus said, 'everything is possible for you. Take this cup from me. Yet not what I will, but what you will.'

Mark 14, verse 36.

ACTIVITIES

READING TIME

In Psalm 130, verses 5-6 you can read of someone who had to wait on God.

TALKING TIME

Do you ever make plans to do something and then tell your mum or dad your plan and they say no?
How do you feel?
Why might they say no?
Who knows even better what is best for us?
Do you ever want something but are told to wait?
Why might God want you to wait?

ACTION TIME

Sometimes people say that God's answers to prayer can be like traffic lights. Can you work out what each colour would be?
Draw traffic lights and put in what each colour could stand for.

PRAYER TIME

Thank you God that you always hear my prayers. Help me to remember that you always know what is best for me.
Amen.

Belonging to the church

Questions
65 - 72

65

Question

What is the church?

Answer

The church is made up of all those who belong to Jesus.

The church meets together in a building. The church is not the building, but the people who meet there. Jesus has called them to come to him. They are Jesus' special friends. Because they love Jesus they love each other too. The church is Jesus' family.

Memory Verse

Christ loved the church and gave himself up for her to make her holy.
   Ephesians 5, verses 25-26.

ACTIVITIES

READING TIME

In Hebrews 10, verse 25 you will find a verse about the people of the church meeting together.

TALKING TIME

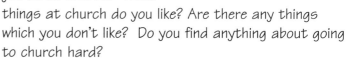

What is your church like? Describe the building where you meet. Who are your favourite people? What do you do at church? What things at church do you like? Are there any things which you don't like? Do you find anything about going to church hard?
What could you do to help in your church?

ACTION TIME

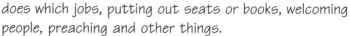

Make a list of any one in your church who has a job to do or find out who does which jobs, putting out seats or books, welcoming people, preaching and other things.
Pray for these people. Is there any you could help?
How can you show love to other Christians?

PRAYER TIME

Lord, thank you that you have given me special friends at church. Help us all to love you and to love each other more. Amen.

Question

What is the church for?

Answer

The church is for loving, serving and praising God, and for helping others to do that too.

Because we love Jesus we want to praise him. We also want to learn more about him. We want to serve him. That is why we meet together and sing about him. We also listen to what his Word, the Bible, has to tell us. Jesus has also given us special signs which we can use to remind us of his love. Because we know how much he loves us we want to tell others about him.

Memory Verse

But you are a chosen people, a royal priesthood, a holy nation, a people belonging to God, that you may declare the praises of him who called you out of darkness into his wonderful light.

1 Peter 2, verse 8.

ACTIVITIES

READING TIME

Read Acts 2, verses 42-47 to find out about the first church.

TALKING TIME

What do you think the early church would have been like? What things are different and what things would be the same today? Talk about the different parts there are to your service.

ACTION TIME

Find out about different churches in other countries. What sort of building do they meet in? Do they have a service like yours? What things are the same in all Christian churches?

PRAYER TIME

Thank you God for our church. Thank you that we can meet to praise you and to learn more about you. Amen.

Question

Why do we sing in church?

Answer

We sing songs to help us to praise God and to pray to him.

Almost everybody likes music and songs. God has made us so that music and songs help us to show we are happy or sad. When we meet together we sing to him. We also sing to each other so that we can tell each other about what God has done. God enjoys our singing and listens to our hearts as well as to our voices.

Memory Verse

Be filled with the Spirit. Speak to one another with psalms, hymns and spiritual songs. Sing and make music in your heart to the Lord.
Ephesians 5, verses 18-19.

ACTIVITIES

Look up Psalms 92, verses 1-3; 144, verse 9; 149, verse 3, to find out about praising God.

TALKING TIME

What is your favourite song you sing in church? Why?
What are you doing when you are singing to God?
Do you have a favourite song from the Book of Psalms?

ACTION TIME

Draw the scene described in Revelation chapters 4 and 5. Can you find space in your picture to write the words of one of the songs in chapter 5?

PRAYER TIME

Dear God, please help me to praise you when I am singing. Teach me what the words I sing really mean.
Amen.

Question

Why is there a sermon when we gather to worship?

Answer

The sermon explains God's Word and helps us to trust and obey him.

Jesus has given a special gift to some people in his church.
They can explain the Bible and help us to obey it.
Jesus uses their sermons to speak to us.
He shows us things that are wrong in our lives. He tells us what he will do for us.
He wants us to learn more about him and to trust him. Make sure you listen to his voice.

Memory Verse

My sheep listen to my voice; I know them, and they follow me.
John 10, verse 27.

ACTIVITIES

READING TIME

Read 1 Corinthians 12, verses 27-29 to find out the different things that some people have gifts for.

TALKING TIME

Who gives the sermon in your church?
How do they know what to say? Why do we need to listen?

ACTION TIME

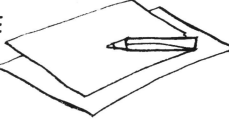

Next time you are in church for the sermon, try very hard to listen to what is said. Maybe you could write down the main points to help you remember.

PRAYER TIME

Dear God, please help me to listen to your voice more in church. Help me not to get distracted and think about other things.
Amen.

Question

Why has Jesus given us special signs to use in the church?

Answer

Jesus has given us special signs as pictures to remind us of his love.

A sign is a message in pictures instead of words. You see signs in the street every day. We also use signs. We shake hands to show we are friends. We clap our hands to show that we are pleased. Some people wag a finger to tell us we have done something wrong! Jesus has given us two special signs, Baptism and the Lord's Supper. His signs tell us that he loves us.

Memory Verse

Having loved his own who were in the world, Jesus now showed them the full extent of his love.
        John 13, verse 1.

ACTIVITIES

READING TIME

Read Exodus 13, verse 20-22 to find another place in the Bible where signs were given.

TALKING TIME

Jesus gave us two special signs, but other signs are used in the Bible too. What other signs mean things for Christians today? Have you seen the fish shape, the cross, or the dove? What do these signs mean?

ACTION TIME

Draw some of the signs above. Can you think of or make up any others too?

PRAYER TIME

Dear God, thank you for the church. Thank you for the special signs that you give to us to remind us of your love.
Amen.

Question

What is the first sign Jesus has given to us?

Answer

The first sign in which Jesus shows his love for us is baptism.

When we are baptised, water comes pouring over us.
The water is a sign that our hearts need to be washed clean from sin. It reminds us that Jesus alone can do that. He died on the cross to wash away our sin. He has promised to wash away the sins of everyone who trusts him. Baptism means: Jesus cleanses sinful hearts – trust him!

Memory Verse

Peter replied, 'Repent and be baptised every one of you, in the name of Jesus Christ for the forgiveness of your sins. And you will receive the gift of the Holy Spirit.'
    Acts 2, verses 38-39.

ACTIVITIES

READING TIME

Read about Jesus' baptism in Matthew 3, verse 13-17.

TALKING TIME

Have you seen a baptism in your church?
What happened?
Why is it so important?
What is the water a sign of?

ACTION TIME

Draw a picture of a baptism you have seen. Find out what promises were made at the service.
Write them underneath your picture.

PRAYER TIME

Dear Jesus, thank you that you can make us clean. Please help me to trust you. Amen.

Question

What is the second sign Jesus has given to us?

Answer

The second sign in which Jesus shows his love for us is the Lord's Supper.

The first Lord's Supper took place on the night Jesus was betrayed. Jesus broke some bread and gave it to his disciples to eat. The broken bread is a sign of the way Jesus' body was broken for our sins. Jesus also gave his disciples a cup of wine to drink. The cup is a sign of the blood Jesus shed on the cross for us. When we come to the Lord's Table, Jesus is with us. When we eat the bread and drink the wine, it is a sign that we trust Jesus and take him as our Saviour and friend.

Memory Verse

For whenever you eat this bread and drink this cup, you proclaim the Lord's death until he comes.
1 Corinthians 11, verse 26.

ACTIVITIES

READING TIME

Read about the first Lord's Supper in Luke 22, verses 14-23.

TALKING TIME

Describe any time you have seen the Lord's Supper or communion taking place. What happened? What does it mean to Christians? What do the bread and wine stand for?

ACTION TIME

In Bible times, God's people ate a special type of bread. Can you find out what it was called and what was different about it?
Read Matthew 26, verses 17-30. Imagine you are one of Jesus' disciples and write your story of what it was like to be there. What did you see and hear?

PRAYER TIME

Dear Lord Jesus, thank you for the sign of the Lord's Supper. Thank you for showing your love to us in this way.
Amen.

Question

How can we help those who do not yet trust and love Jesus?

Answer

We can help them by telling them the good news about Jesus.

Jesus is the only Saviour. He wants our friends to hear that he can be their Saviour too. We can tell our friends about him. We can pray that those who have never heard about him will hear soon. We can help those who go to tell others about Jesus. Perhaps Jesus will want us to go to another country to tell others about his love. But first we must tell the friends we already have at home.

Memory Verse

Go and make disciples of all nations . . . teaching them to obey everything I have commanded you. And surely I am with you always, to the very end of the age.
    Matthew 28, verses 19-20.

ACTIVITIES

READING TIME

Read Romans 10, verse 14 to discover how we can help those who haven't heard about Jesus.

TALKING TIME

Have you ever told a friend about Jesus? Did you find it easy or hard? Think about what you might say to them. What are the really important things to say about Jesus?

ACTION TIME

Pray about someone you could talk to about Jesus.
Find out about someone who has gone to another place to tell people about Jesus.
Get a map and find out exactly where they are. Pray for them too.

PRAYER TIME

Dear Lord, sometimes I find it hard to tell my friends about you. Please give me courage to speak and the words to say.
Amen.

Jesus will come back

Questions
73 - 77

Question

Will Jesus be with us always?

Answer

Jesus promised that he would be with us always and especially when we are telling others about him.

Jesus is with us everywhere we go. He will be with us to the end of time. He promises to be near us when we speak to others about him. He knows that it is difficult. He knows we are sometimes afraid of what people will say or do. He knows we sometimes worry that we may lose our friends. But he is our best friend. We will never lose him. Jesus will never leave anyone who trusts him.

Memory Verse

One night the Lord spoke to Paul in a vision: 'Do not be afraid; keep on speaking, do not be silent. For I am with you.'
Acts 18, verses 9-10.

ACTIVITIES

READING TIME

In Matthew 28, verses 16-20 you will find the promise that Jesus gave to the disciples.

TALKING TIME

What does it mean to make a promise? Have you ever made a promise to someone? Did you manage to keep it? Will you always manage to keep every promise that you make? Did Jesus ever break his promises? What special promise did Jesus make to us that we should remember when we try to tell others about him?

ACTION TIME

The rainbow is a special sign given by God to show that he will keep a special promise. Can you find out what this promise was? (Genesis 9, verses 1-17.) Paint or use colour pencils to create a large rainbow. To remind you of God's faithfulness write, 'God always keeps his promises.'

PRAYER TIME

Dear Lord Jesus, thank you that you never break your promises to us. Help me to be more willing to talk to people about you.
Amen.

74

Question

When will the end of the age take place?

Answer

The end of the age will take place when the Lord Jesus returns.

God has not told us when the world will end.
But he has told us that one day Jesus will come back.
Jesus will return as King and Judge. Everyone will bow down before him. He will change everything to the way things should be. He will make a new world out of the old one. Then everything will be just right.

Memory Verse

He who was seated on the throne said, 'I am making everything new!'
Revelation 21, verse 5.

ACTIVITIES

Read 1 Thessalonians 5, verses 1-2 to find out a little about the end of the age.

TALKING TIME

What sort of things do you think will be different when Jesus comes again? What will there not be?

ACTION TIME

Make a poster with the title 'When Jesus Comes Back'.
Make it of all the words you can think of which describe what the world will be like.
Make the words big and bright!

PRAYER TIME

Dear God, thank you that you have everything planned perfectly and that you know when Jesus will return. Thank you that everything will be made new then. Amen.

75

Question

What will happen when Jesus comes back?

Answer

Those who love Jesus will go to be with him, but others will be sent away from his presence forever. If we trust and love Jesus we will be with him forever!

We will be able to see him. We will join all those who have trusted and loved him. Jesus called this 'heaven'.

But those who have not wanted Jesus as their Saviour will not be with him. The Bible tells us they will be in the darkness outside. They will never see him.

Memory Verse

In my Father's house are many rooms; if it were not so I would have told you. I am going there to prepare a place for you.
        John 14, verse 2.

ACTIVITIES

READING TIME

In Luke 16, verse 19-31 Jesus talks about what happened to someone who died.

TALKING TIME

Have you ever lost someone or something? How did you feel? Talk about the fact that those who do not know God will be separated from him forever.

ACTION TIME

Do you know anyone who has lost a friend or relative, through death recently? Is there anything you can do to bring them comfort and show that you care for them?

PRAYER TIME

Dear Lord Jesus, you have taught us that you alone can bring us to heaven. Thank you for your love. Help me to tell others about you so that they will trust you.
Amen.

Question

Why do we die?

Answer

We die because of sin.

We have sin in our hearts from the very beginning of our lives. When we sin we turn away from God.

Because of that our bodies will not last forever. We all die because sin is present in all of our lives.

But when Jesus comes he will bring both sin and death to an end. Then those who trust Jesus will never leave his presence. But those who do not trust him will never see his face again.

Memory Verse

For the wages of sin is death, but the gift of God is eternal life in Christ Jesus our Lord.
Romans 6, verse 23.

ACTIVITIES

READING TIME

In 1 Corinthians 15, verses 55-57 you can read more about sin and death.

TALKING TIME

What do you think sin is? Has sin always been in our lives? What will Jesus do to sin when he comes back?

ACTION TIME

Read Revelation chapter 21, verse 9 to chapter 22, verse 5.
Can you draw a poster of this scene? Make a list of the things you will need to put in the picture before you begin.

PRAYER TIME

Dear Lord Jesus, thank you that you have the power to bring sin and death to an end. Thank you that if we trust you we will always be with you.
Amen.

Question

What will it be like to be with Jesus forever?

Answer

All those who love Jesus will be with him and will enjoy the new heavens and the new earth.

Jesus will make a new world, where everything is perfect. There will be no sin, no tears, no sadness, no death. There will be eternal life! Everyone there will be a friend of Jesus, and our friend too. Jesus will give us new things to do to show that we belong to him. We will be with our Saviour and with all those who love him. It will be a time of perfect happiness that will never end.

Memory **V**erse

I will come back and take you to be with me.

John 14, verse 3.

ACTIVITIES

READING TIME

Read 2 Peter 3, verse 13 and 2 Timothy 4, verse 18 and find out what we can look forward to.

TALKING TIME

What can we look forward to about heaven?
What will we do?
Think about what heaven will mean to some people in your church.
Will it ever end?

ACTION TIME

Think about an event or outing you are looking forward to. Do you have to make any preparations before you go?
In what ways can you get ready to meet Jesus?

PRAYER TIME

Dear Jesus, thank you that one day all those who trust you will see you in heaven. I want to see you! Help me to trust you every day of my life from now on.
Amen.

INDEX OF QUESTIONS

If you have enjoyed this book from Christian Focus Publications, you may be interested to read other titles by Sinclair B Ferguson.

The Big Book of Questions & Answers about Jesus

In this book, Sinclair Ferguson focuses on the person and work of Jesus. A great resource for parents and teachers.

ISBN 978-1-85792-559-3

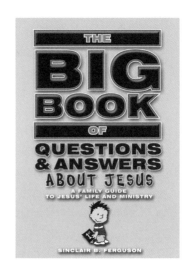

Sinclair Ferguson investigates God's word and the life of Jesus to find out the answers to fascinating questions. How are we to become wise? How should we pray? How do we become happy? How can we be good? Find out the answers, as taught by Jesus, in this imaginative and fun series.

Jesus teaches us how to be Happy
ISBN 978-1-85792-981-2
Jesus teaches us how to be Wise
ISBN 978-1-85792-982-9
Jesus teaches us how to Pray
ISBN 978-1-85792-984-3
Jesus teaches us how to be Good
ISBN 978-1-85792-983-6

For more information contact Christian Focus Publications, Geanies House, Fearn, Tain, Ross-shire, IV20 1TW, Scotland, U.K.
Tel: +44 (0) 1862 871011. Fax: +44 (0) 1862 871699
E-mail: info@christianfocus.com   www.christianfocus.com

THE BIG BOOK OF BIBLE TRUTHS
Volumes 1 and 2

You can never have too many stories! Children love them. We all do! And who better to hear about in a story than the great storyteller himself, Jesus.

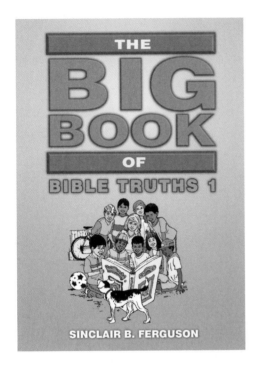

Through the stories in this book you will find out about Jesus, his life and how he wants to get to know you. Sinclair tells twenty-seven stories that will teach you about what it means to be a Christian.

Nick-names, moth burgers – there are many interesting stories that teach you things you didn't know before and loads of cool stuff about Jesus Christ, the Son of God.

Illustrated throughout, this book is going to be another family favourite! Includes Extra Features: Bible reading; lesson summary; prayer.

ISBN: 978-1-84550-371-0

Here are another twenty-seven stories that will teach you about what it means to belong to God's family. There are lots of different people to discover, including an architect and a master craftsman. You will also be able to work out what a revival is and if Jesus' mum ever got in a tizzy.

Sinclair tells many interesting stories that will teach you things you didn't know before. God, Jesus and You – what a team! Now that's a winning combination – no doubt about it!

There are illustrations throughout the book, so it's all set to be another of your family's favourites! Includes Extra Features: Bible reading; lesson summary; prayer.

ISBN: 978-1-84550-372-7

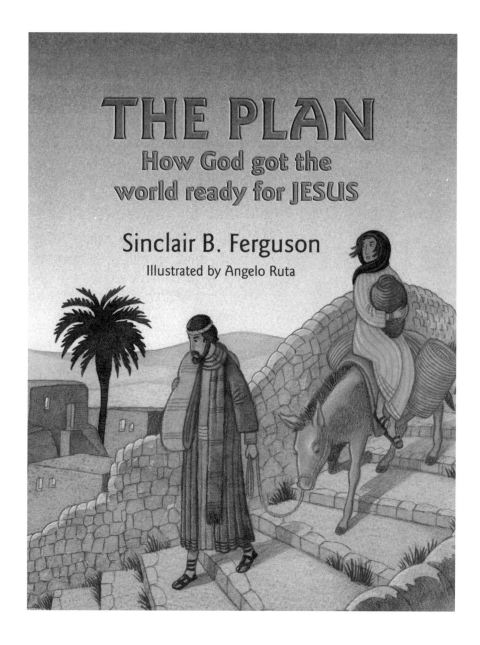

Before the dawn of time a plan was made, a plan to save and a plan to love, a plan to rescue and a plan to send. One after the other, people were sent to be where they were needed to be.

In the distance, wise men ride camels through the desert. A star glimmers in the night sky. They have a long way to go and many months of travel ahead of them.

Some shepherds stand guard over their flock of sheep as a young couple struggle the last few miles of a tiring journey desperate for shelter and a place to sleep.

All have been sent to one place for one event that will change the world forever. The one and only Saviour of the world will be born that night in a stable, in a little country called Israel, in a little town called Bethlehem.

The key part of the plan is a baby and his name will be Jesus, for he will save his people from their sins.

ISBN: 978-1-84550-451-9

THE AUTHOR

Sinclair B. Ferguson is Senior Minister of First Presbyterian Church, Columbia. He is also Distinguished Visiting Professor of Systematic Theology at Westminister Theological Seminary. He was formerly minister of St. George's-Tron Church in Glasgow. In addition to his regular work he speaks and writes extensively on the Christian faith. His books are written out of a conviction that biblical teaching builds strong Christians; a number of his works are available in several languages.

Sinclair and Dorothy Ferguson have four children of their own. Like all parents they know the challenges that face families today. Realising how difficult it can be to find reliable books to help children understand the Christian faith, Dr Ferguson has written
The Big Book of Questions and Answers.
It is designed to:

- Help children and their parents and teachers to understand the Bible.
  - To talk about the Bible naturally.
- Grow strong in their own faith in a world of tremendous spiritual
  - and moral confusion and uncertainty.

CHRISTIAN FOCUS PUBLICATIONS

Christian Focus | Christian Heritage | CF4K | Mentor

Christian Focus Publications publishes books for adults and children under its four main imprints: Christian Focus, CF4K, Mentor and Christian Heritage. Our books reflect that God's word is reliable and Jesus is the way to know him, and live for ever with him.

Our children's publication list includes a Sunday school curriculum that covers pre-school to early teens; puzzle and activity books. We also publish personal and family devotional titles, biographies and inspirational stories that children will love.

If you are looking for quality Bible teaching for children then we have an excellent range of Bible story and age specific theological books.

From pre-school to teenage fiction, we have it covered!

Find us at our web page:
www.christianfocus.com